YOU CAN DRAW
CONSTRUCTION VEHICLES

by Mattia Cerato

PICTURE WINDOW BOOKS
a capstone imprint

MATERIALS

Before you start your amazing drawings, there are a few things you'll need.

pencil

colored pencils

markers

paper

eraser

ruler

SHAPES

Drawing can be easy! In fact, if you can draw these simple letters, numbers, shapes, and lines, YOU CAN DRAW anything in this book.

letters

D S L U
V Z

numbers

1 2 3

shapes

lines

FORKLIFT

POWER SHOVEL

CRANE TRUCK

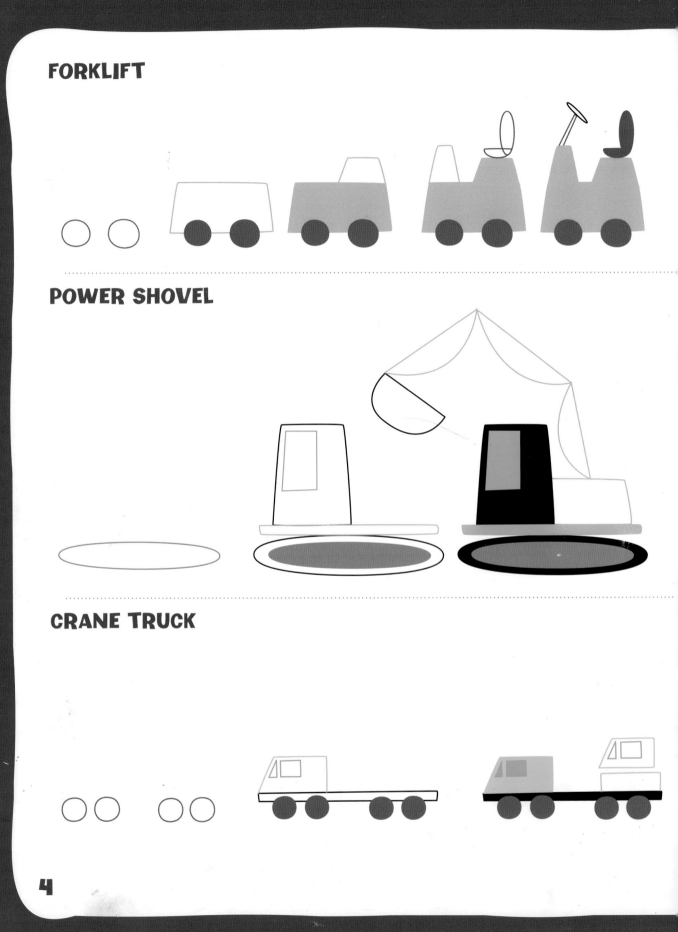

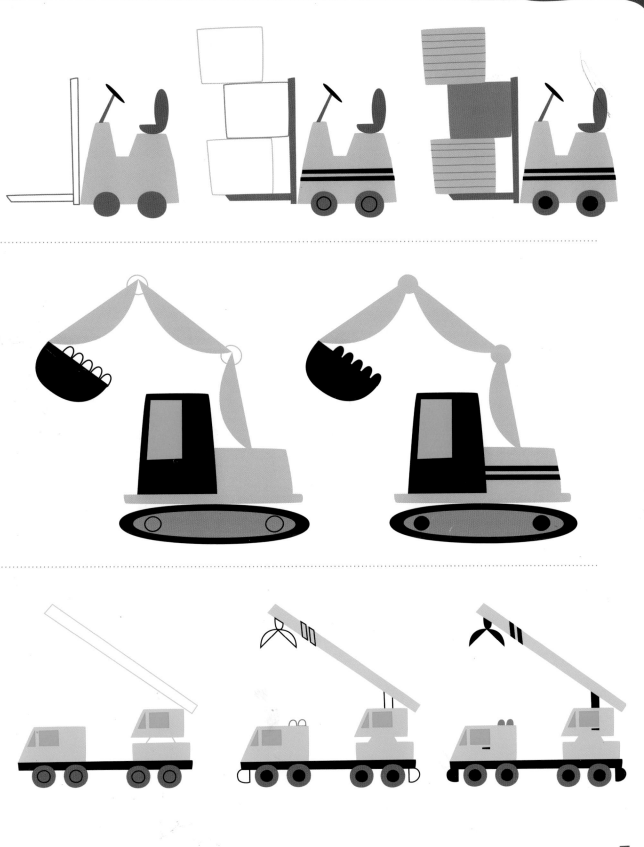

CEMENT TRUCK

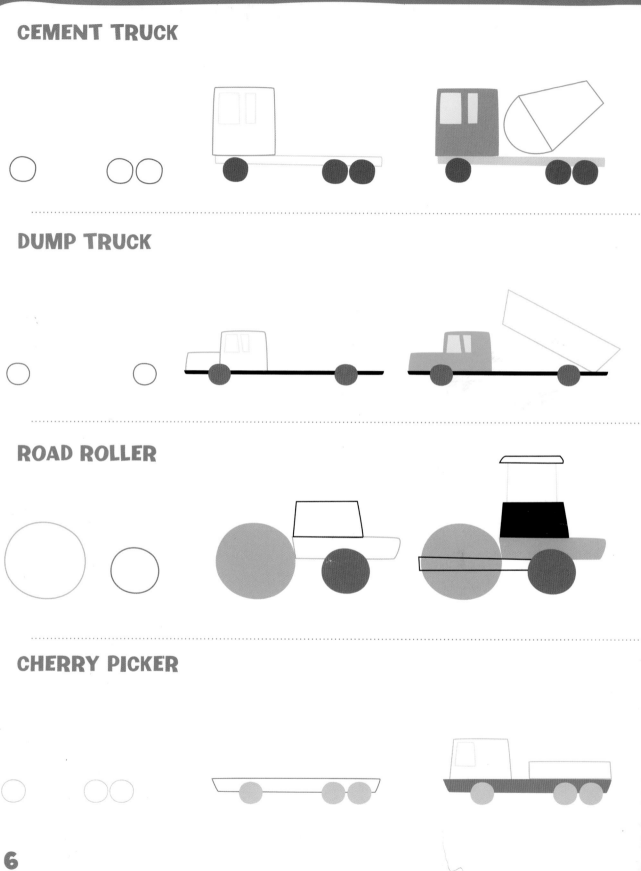

DUMP TRUCK

ROAD ROLLER

CHERRY PICKER

BACKHOE

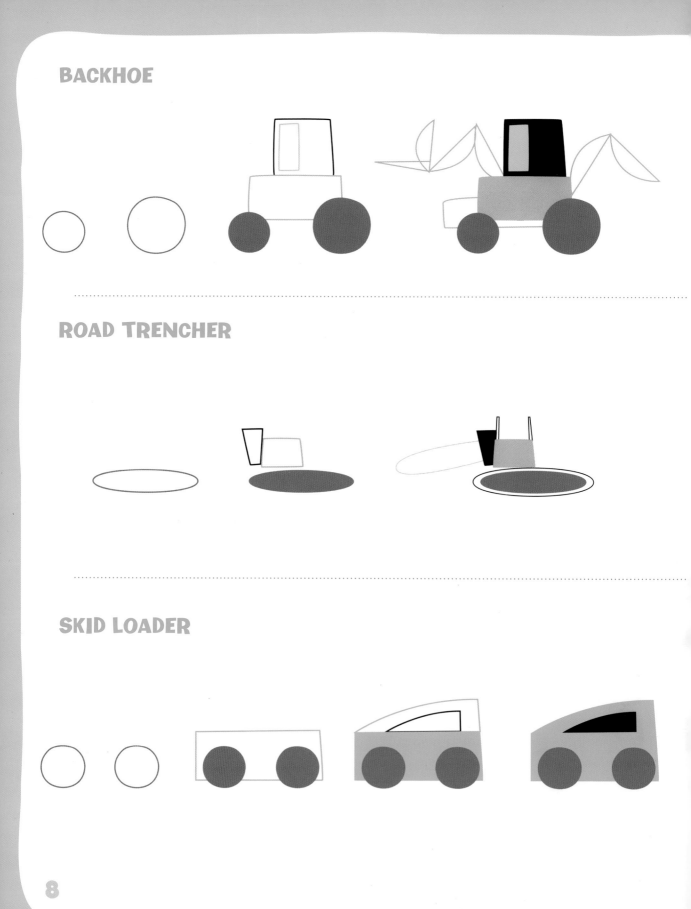

ROAD TRENCHER

SKID LOADER

MEGA DUMP TRUCK

HELICOPTER CRANE

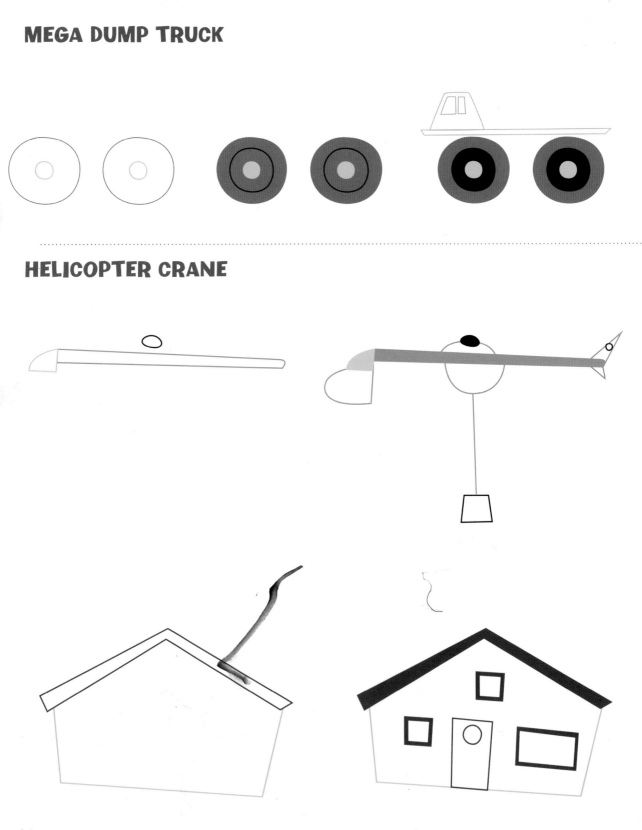

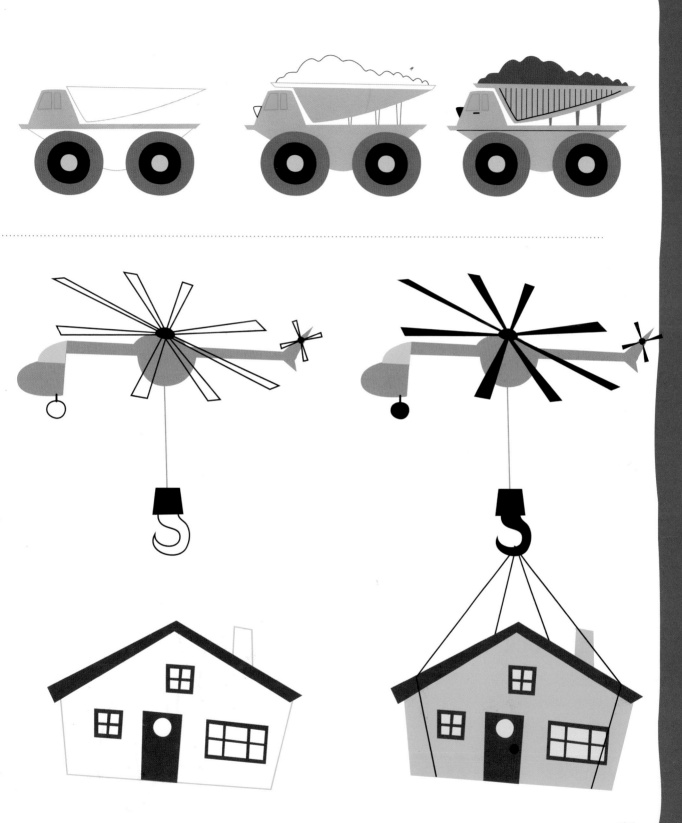

BULLDOZER

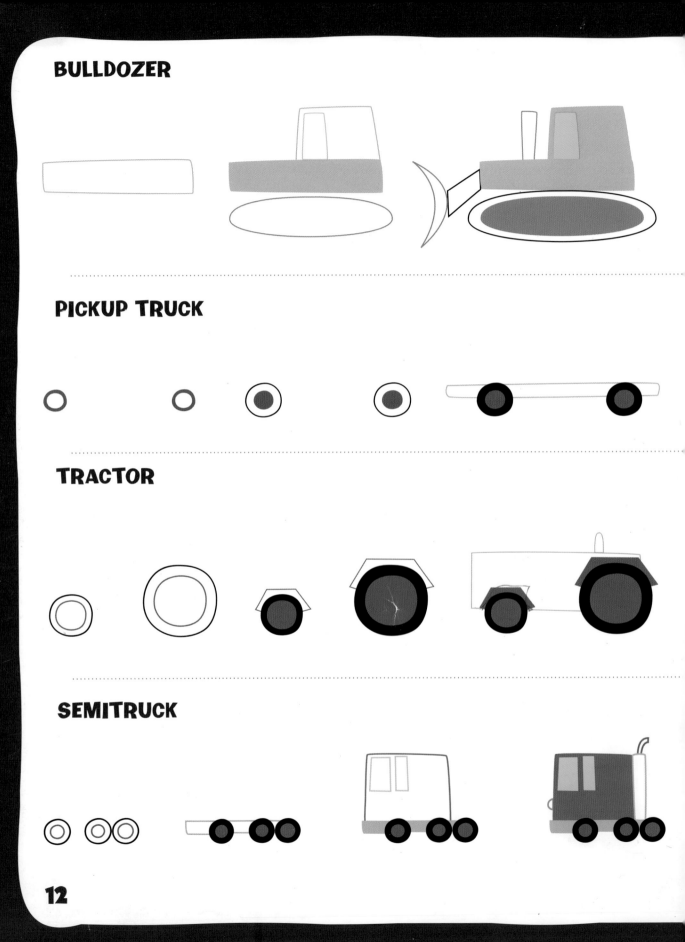

PICKUP TRUCK

TRACTOR

SEMITRUCK

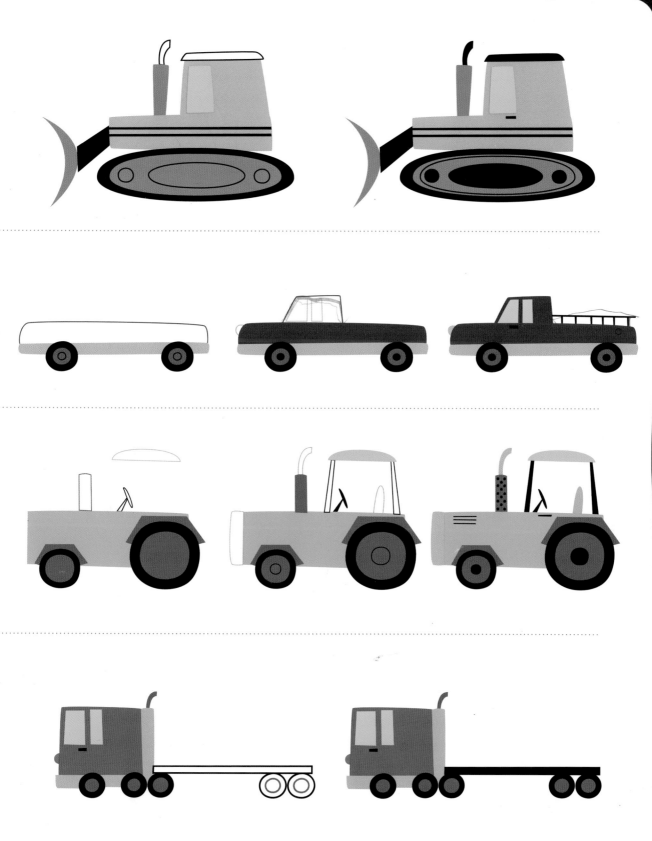

FELLER BUNCHER

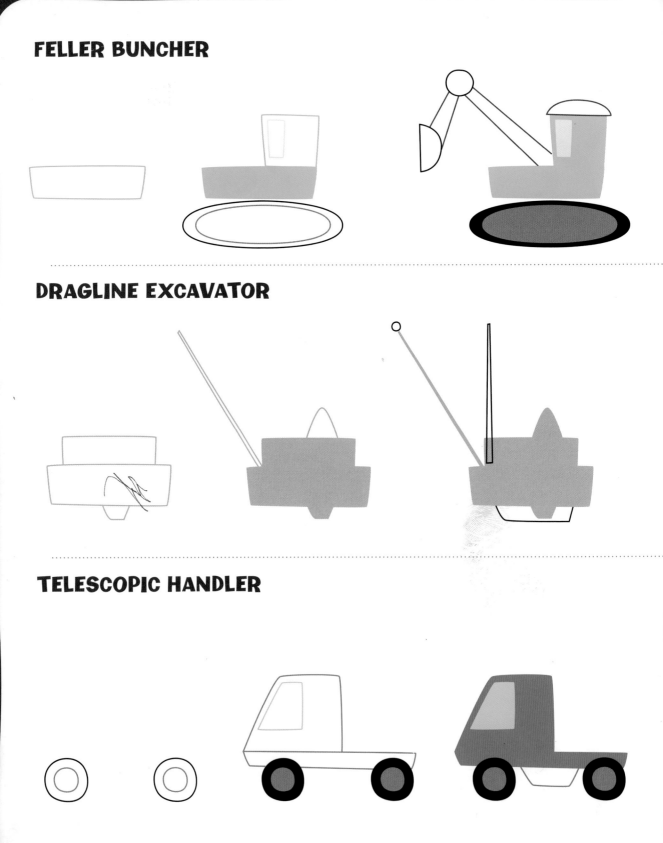

DRAGLINE EXCAVATOR

TELESCOPIC HANDLER

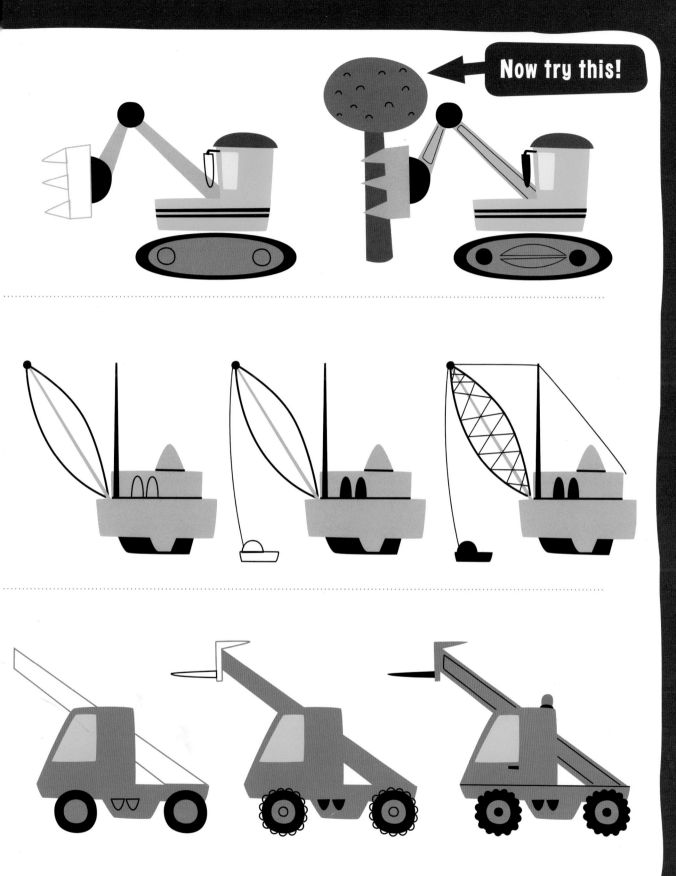

15

BLADE LEVELER

SUCTION EXCAVATOR

COLD PLANER

ARTICULATED TRUCK

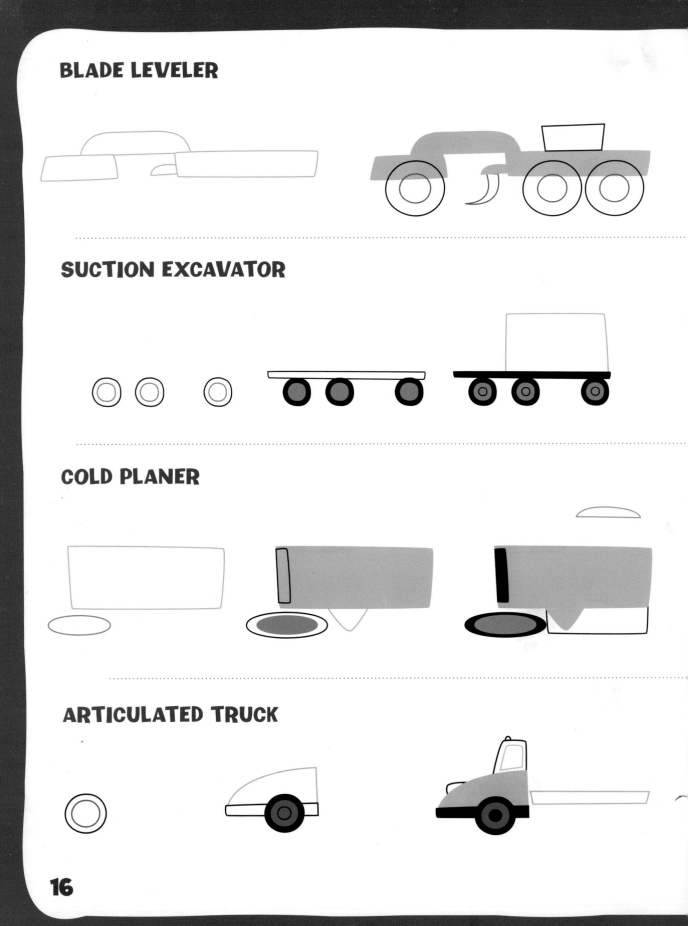

16

SCISSOR LIFT

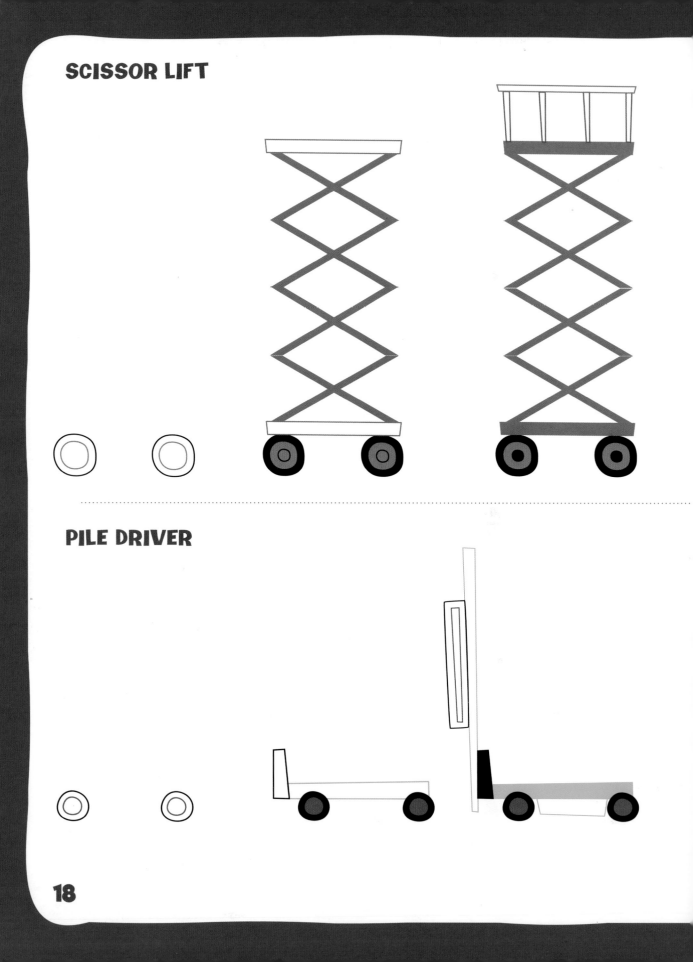

PILE DRIVER

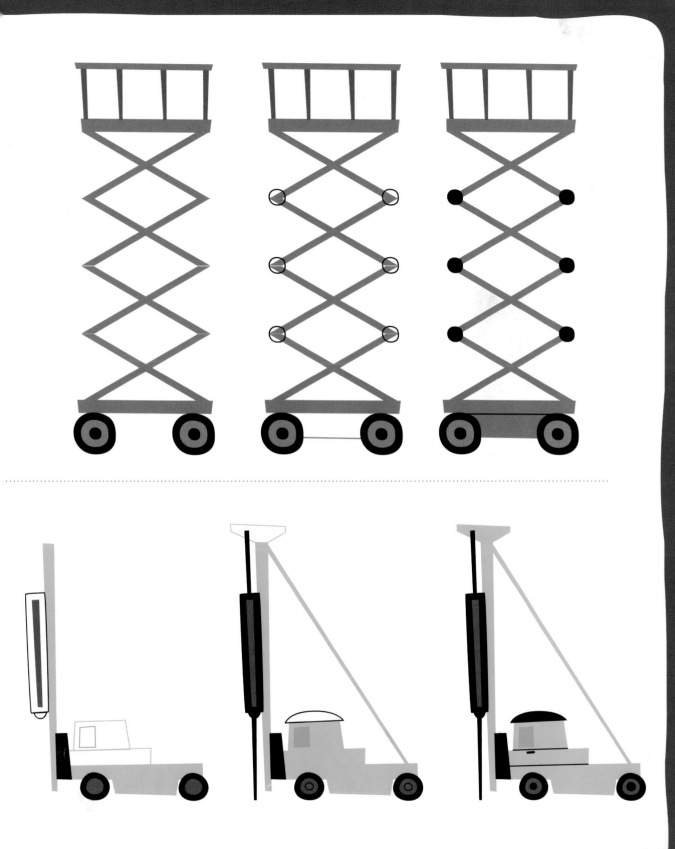

BARRICADE

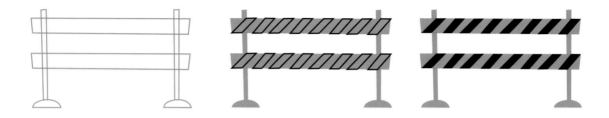

SAFETY CONES

HARD HAT

CABLE SPOOL

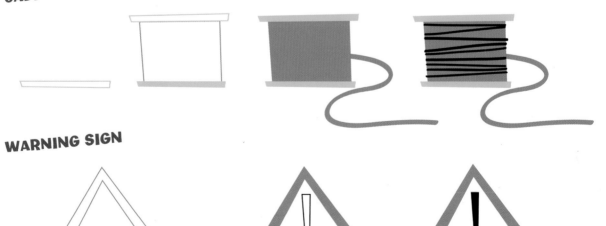

WARNING SIGN

JACKHAMMER

HAMMER

SAW

ROCKS

DRILL

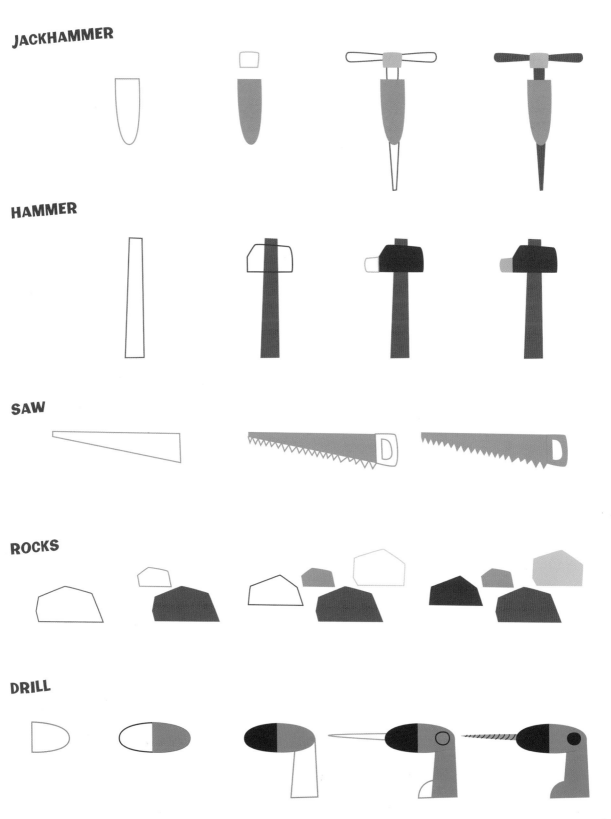

23

Library of Congress Cataloging-in-Publication Data
Cerato, Mattia.
 You can draw construction vehicles / by Mattia Cerato.
   p. cm. — (You can draw)
 ISBN 978-1-4048-6807-6 (library binding)
 1. Motor vehicles in art—Juvenile literature. 2.
Drawing—Technique—Juvenile literature. 3. Construction
equipment—Juvenile literature. I. Title. II. Series.

NC825.M64C47 2012
743'.89629225—dc22   2011006999

Printed in the United States of America in North Mankato, Minnesota.
032011   006110CGF11

Picture Window Books
151 Good Counsel Drive
P.O. Box 669
Mankato, MN 56002-0669
877-845-8392
www.capstonepub.com

Editor: Shelly Lyons
Designer: Matt Bruning
Art Director: Nathan Gassman
Production Specialist: Sarah Bennett
The illustrations in this book were created digitally.

Internet Sites •

FactHound offers a safe, fun way to find Internet sites related to this book.
All of the sites on FactHound have been researched by our staff.

Here's all you do:

Visit *www.facthound.com*

Type in this code: 9781404868076

Check out projects, games and lots more at
www.capstonekids.com

Look for all the books in the **You Can Draw** series:

YOU CAN DRAW
CONSTRUCTION VEHICLES

YOU CAN DRAW DINOSAURS

YOU CAN DRAW
DRAGONS, UNICORNS,
AND OTHER
MAGICAL CREATURES

YOU CAN DRAW
FAIRIES
AND **PRINCESSES**

YOU CAN DRAW MONSTERS
AND OTHER
SCARY THINGS

YOU CAN DRAW
PETS